QUATRAINS

First Edition

Illustrated by: Tina Nusu

A Green Leaf Publishing Book

The Quatrains of Christopher B. Douglas
Copyright © 1995, 1996 by C. B. Douglas

First Printing 1997

ISBN 0-9660521-0-2

Library of Congress Catalog Card Number: 97-94521

Except as permitted under the United States Copyright Act of 1976, no part of this publication may be reproduced or distributed in any form or by any means, or stored in a data base or retrieval system, without the prior written permission from the publisher.

Printed in the United States of America
10 9 8 7 6 5 4 3 2 1

Green Leaf Publishing Co. • Box 73247 • Las Vegas NV 89170-3247
• (702) 594-1455

Acknowledgments

Special thanks to the few people who helped making this book possible: my priceless parents John and Constance Douglas, for their continuous encouragement and endorsement, my lovely wife Ioana, for her enlivening support and commitment, rendered as I am passing through perhaps the most difficult time in my life, and to Tina Nusu, for the earnest support she provided by designing the delicate, expressive art illustrations in a timeless and dedicated manner.

From the Author

Long ago, when December snow flurries danced over a town called Bucharest, John Douglas, my father, sitting next to a chimney, was narrating a few rubaiyats from the Persian, Omar Khayyam. At the end, he asked me what I thought of Khayyam's philosophy.
" Unique", I responded.
"Others may have gathered the stones, but Omar put them together and laid the foundation, setting the 'table' for all that followed, to write on", he replied.
After 35 years, one eve I sat down and wrote a verse:

"Khayyam, you fooled me my old friend
When said, you'll go and *"that's the End"*
Last night, while writing, as a Sign
You helped my verse and poured me wine."

It seemed like my pen was just writing without me, for a day before some unusual rimes came out, and it appeared so easy to scrawl. And the thoughts resembled fragments of our everyday life, and instants of someone's knowledge, like yours, reflecting restfully over and over upon the pages, which follow herein.

Yours is the judgment written here and yours is the image enclosed. I get no merit for anything, but I've been reserved the satisfaction of a *"thought collector"*.

Nothing looks more appealing than one's very images, all put together in a volume format, but when opened, revealing an unmatched infinity. In within yourselves there are no boundaries, unless are created, and wherever you may be, however you may feel, you should always have these refrains nearby, and if you feel lonesome, I promise to return whenever my name is called and so I remain,
Eternally yours,
EXANTUS

"Reality only reveals itself when is illuminated by a ray of poetry."
Georges Braque
(1882-1963)

Once, the *Queen of Hearts* and ' *Princess of the World*

Has left beyond a World of Young and a World of Old,

With Her she took the smiles of a Thousand Queens,

Leaving far behind the Ages, of the *Past* and *Cold*.

(In remembrance of HRH Diana, Princess of Wales)

1.

With every day that passes by

A young man's born, an old man dies,

And thousand stars await its turn

To go, and never to return...

2.

Enjoy the minute of Today

Tomorrow, it maybe too late,

For Life and Death are old time friends

And endless games they like to play.

3.

To Sing and Play and Love and Breathe,

To Sleep and Eat and to Enjoy

The Life that's given – not a toy

To be amused of – *Careful Please!*

4.

A woman of your dreams in a Garden of Eden,

A Tree of Knowledge and a fruit forbidden;

Beware though – The Thirst of Lore at the Sight of Love

Has nailed the Ten Commandments way *down* and *Above*.

5.

For here I come to see the World

Rotate its ways and Life unfold,

And One-Way only does it move

And I with it, so I was told...

6.

Do not forget my dear friend

From Earth you came and shall descend,

Except for Him who had arrived

From other Worlds where there's no end.

7.

And when you'll realize you're Old and Gray

Rewind your thoughts to *that* regretting day

And call my name, and I in spirit form, descending

Shall whisper in your ear: - I love You, to a never ending! ...

8.

Don't question *Why*, but try to be

Yourself, with many lonely dreams,

Where memories come back and stay

And thousand years a minute seems...

The Clock is ticking, every second: *Snip*!
For every moment passed, one more to whip,
The *Time Inventor* never had defined
When not awake, where do these seconds *Sleep*?

Whatever you may choose: the *Right* or *Wrong*
Your *Book of Life* when finished, shall belong
To the *Eternal Library*, entire *Chapters All*,
In favor of the *Master of your Soul*.

9.

Your Walks and Figure shall attract attention

And all desire your body to enjoy

To Love and Play and Kiss and Pull and Reap

And then, to leave your heart an empty deep.

10.

Twist and twine, the Life is winding

And we seem so far away

And yet so close to the *Final Answer*

Which divides the Night and Day.

11.

As I retreated in the fields

I heard a *Thunder-Voice* and confused

Looked up from where the calling came:

" *Don't play with Fire, you shall lose! ...* "

12.

To love in dreams and then to keep

The ever loved forever near,

You shall awake and search in fear

A hopeless search, of timeless deep.

13.

Young, much too young I had to be to fall

For that pretended *Infinite* in which we roll;

Disgusted now I watch the flying years

Betray my love for life and steal it all.

14.

Forget the Stress, the Problems and the Grief

And let your body floating like a leaf,

The Wind shall sway you to your *Destined Lane*,

Ignore the Strain, the Problems and the Pain.

15.

Look in the mirror and watch the Time

Running backwards... What a scold!

For in your Image you may feel

You're getting young while getting old! ...

16.

As I embraced this woman with Desire

Her ways have conquered of my soul entire

And in those moments, happily have I thrown

A World of Great Importance, into fire...

17.

From high above and far away

They see a World rotate its Rotten

And to their callow they convey

What constellation had forgotten.

18.

You're Born. Observe. You Play. You Grow;

You Learn. You Touch. You feel. You Know;

You like. You think. You Taste. You Try,

You Love. You Worry. Create and Die.

19.

"Confused? And so am I, - Confused!

But never lost my love and hope;

When Life is getting rough and slope

About my end I am amused. -

20.

The chestnut trees and lilacs in bloom

Near your window open, to shadow your room;

A woman to love, a bosom to roll;

A perfect combination of Body and Soul.

21.

enerations! Generations

Young at heart – "Where did they run?"

Future hopes and Revelations,

Thoughtful minds – "Where have you gone? "

22.

Before reincarnation the Soul had simply asked

For one more imaginary second into the Universe to last,

And from the whole Eternity where all Creation lives and lie'

He looked upon the Puzzling Earth and into flesh was born to die.

23.

"What is God? – I'd be a fool to say for certain;

For no one ever came from where they went behind that curtain,

But I could tell you this, my dear friend: -" By heart and mind,

To find Him, you must first look into you, yourself to find...

24.

Don't Lie. Don't Scoff. Don't Hate. Don't Kill;

Don't rape. Don't Hit someone. Don't Envy and don't Steal;

Don't Boast. Don't look for Fame, nor do your passions treasure,

Don't sell your Soul, your heart, your body, for a passing pleasure.

25.

Help them anytime you can,

Smile at Destiny now and then,

Build up Goals and Sweet believes

And then, let go like Autumn's leaves.

26.

A "Friend" you need, but who's to say

Who by your side a lifetime be,

When you betrayed by Destiny

Will kneel down and simply Pray?

The *Optimist* and *Pessimist* argue again
Whether the glass is *Full* or *Empty* halfway in,
And so they asked another as to pick a side
And have been told: " *He, who drinks from it, is to decide* ".

One starry evening as I sat on my porch chair,
I thought I heard a mocking bird singing a Prayer;
Astonished as I was, she said: " My Dear
I only Sing for those who Want to Hear! "

27.

You're nothing but a *Motion Image*

A *Film* that's played a different way,

A story ending like all stories;

Wherefore *new* actors come and play...

28.

It seems as if so far beyond and long ago

We left those moments of our passion'd loving so;

The *thread* which splits reality from real dreams,

Divides our lives forever, though it seems... -

29.

You'll add my name to your *forgotten list*

As if we've never met and I do not exist;

The dreams we've dreamed together, water thinned,

Shall blow from our memories, just like wind.

30.

Afraid of Life you followed up you Mother

And into this Dimension you arrived in Pain;

" Afraid of an after-world existence? Why, don't bother! ;

Wherever she will go, you'll follow her again. "

31.

Life, is but an eyelash tremble

Whereby you and I have met,

You the pen and I the poet

Wrote a page and left so humble.

32.

But, page by page upcoming days you turn,

Your *life-book* getting thin between the covers,

From what you learned you'll teach unto the others

And then depart. And then depart, forlorn...

33.

Imagine you, into this Universe, created,

Born in a World with millions of your kind,

So lonely and of tears desiccated,

Wanting a matching soul, you never seem to find.

34.

Think! *before* you're shaking hands,

And Guard yourself unto defense,

For it could be the friend you need

Is far behind a friend indeed.

35.

Before my Mother lovely girls have sat

To pledge their love for I, but I have not

In their dreams had seem to quench a thirst

Of locking-in a marriage, now forgot...

36.

Revolves the World so many a times

Regardless of its surface' toil;

And men were born to Build and Spoil

Where God Himself in landscape *Signs*.

37.

elf-Destruction: Genocide.

Wars and Violence: Human Pride.

World's Creation? What is it for?

Who re-writes the Future, God to Ignore?

38.

And so, up to the end, the very end,

You'll shuffle thoughts and still not understand

How our Days and Nights have learned to share the sky

And still be different every day than you and I.

39.

See the Blind? The blind can see

Where you'll never reach to be;

You shall never go that deep

While awake or while asleep.

40.

"Khayyam! You fooled me my old friend

When said you'll go and "that's the End";

Last night while writing as a sign

You helped my verse and poured me wine.

41.

One, humbly asked a Priest about and where to mark

The Line which splits *forever* the Daylight from the Dark;

" Within your very chamber your life illuminate,

Before your Night is falling, before it is too late! "

42.

When someone said that *Friendship weighs more than gold,*

One man when heard it, immediately has sold

The only friend he had, and tried to buy again

Another friend, but when announce it, no one showed.

43.

Should you be lost behind your very senses

When those blue eyes encourage your embraces,

Beware though, their glare could be vicious

For it could brake your heart in thousand wishes...

44.

For Medicine, to oust the stress

You'll make a cake of Life and Dine

And burn a candle for each mess

You feel you're in, than share some wine.

45.

The Optimist and Pessimist argue again

Whether the Glass is Full or Empty halfway in,

And so they asked another to pick a side

And have been told: " He, who drinks from it, has to decide. "

46.

Glides the moon upon the waters

And the night is falling deep,

Rest yourself and leave all problems

Far behind and sound asleep.

47.

Whatever you may choose: The Right or Wrong

Your *Book of Life* when finished, shall belong

To the Eternal Library, entire chapters all,

In favor of the Master of your Soul.

48.

Outside the house is snowing so heavenly and slow

And by the fireplace our moods we gently lay;

And let the heat of love into our hearts to blow,

And then, *Ten Thousand Years passed, Today*...

49.

Your Flesh and Body anon shall disappear,

But don't be marked with wondering of fear,

Look up for Love and *find* your Paradise,

And your immortal being will learn to share the skies.

50.

The Prophets and the Saints have told

Unto the Youngsters and the Old

About how ' *"Future"* would one day, become

The highest Commodity ever sold.

The water trickled from the fountain ' crest
Along with thousand years which passed to rest;
"How many lovers by its side set voiceless hopes
Of memories and kissing lips forever pressed?"

The *Woman's Sculpture* made of pallid clay
Was finished by the artist that same day;
"Who's *nude* is that? - I asked him, and She moaned:
" I'm *Venus*...and... Don't touch me... Get away! ..."

51.

You see, a lifetime you must play and act

The fashion that is laid for you in and about,

For there's a Drama or some Parody there is

To dress your *symbol* in some absurd tease.

52.

The one you love, shall play in self-defense

The lover's game of Sweet Impertinence,

And like your shadow back and forth shall run

From you and after you, the more you churn.

53.

After the rain and thunder we shall expect the sun

To wrap in warming wonder the grieving of the woods,

And then, an unknown painter shall frame the doleful moods

In some immortal masterpiece, noticed after he's gone.

54.

Remorsefully, the one that you have chiefly trusted,

Will show you how your confidence has rusted,

Will lay your friendship on a *Scale of Time*

And sell you briefly and with comfort, for a *dime*.

55.

Warm summer and green fields

When Autumn gently builds

A mood for Winter Sorrows

You'll hope for Spring to-morrows.

56.

The Clown's expression *is* what indeed you see

But there is not what it may seem to be,

'Cause there's the truth who hides in funny light

To lay a show for you at 'Circus Night'.

57.

The people ruled by One Man and a few

Shall be the witness' of a war, anew,

The peaceful splendor of the Lands shall turn to horror

While you will fight for WHAT and die for WHO?

58.

A Hope they say, is more than morning light

Which scares the Darkness out of sable night,

And turns the idol sands to one's desires,

Where ' Future Dreams will Conquer and the Past Retires.

59.

One starry evening as I sat on my porch chair

I thought I heard a mocking bird singing a Prayer

Astonished as I was she said, " My Dear!

I only sing for *those* who want to hear!

60.

When Fate, so graciously and dormant shall arrive to choice

Calling your name in soundless, canon and muffled voice,

You shall depart so barren and without possessions

To meet a *Timeless Future* and *Past Generations*.

61.

Somewhere, that *special one* is waiting up for you,

While drowsy thoughts may drive your pace way through,

Don't search for her in vain, awake and stare,

Since you may pass by her while she *is* there.

62.

"Who has equipped your body so full and sans defects

To tempt the very senses, while passionate love erects

For stormy 'n' yet so gentle caresses and desire

That changed the Trail of History and Sinned a World entire?"

63.

Leave the haunting misery and the gloomy stress

For the *Time of Torment* will arrive no less

Than the twilight glare of the destined night

Booked in Eternity by the *Emperor of Light*.

64.

The Infinite, as laid by Nature must I guess,

Is no more that wild, scattered, fireballs of stress,

Where the *Energies of Silence* FIGHT for ever vacant space,

To win *more infinite* and You! Oh, Pre-Destined Human Race.

65.

"For what is Life without a charming chance

Of a New Adventure or Romance?

Oh! Threats of Failure and Hopes of Victory, you incite,

The shy admirers for a Passion Night ".

66.

Lo and Behold! The one who hears well

Shall hear the Tongue of Heaven and the Threats of Hell,

Delimiting the high sounds from the low,

Adopting to its Music and its Show.

67.

Life is for Living, for *only once* you live here, they say,

So make the very best of every second, every day,

Breathe deeply and Imagine you are breathing Life,

The sacred gift once given, let not be pushed away.

68.

Some lovers their Names and Hearts inscribe

Upon a young tree trunk, 'Forever to Survive'

Their marks, long after they depart shall grow

Until no sign of them, or any sign of any tree will ever show.

69.

Right when you're almost there, on that top, you'll fall

And in the hands of Providence you'll rest your hopes and goals

And when you're just about of giving up, an unseen hand

Shall pull your dead weight, back to where you stand.

70.

"To the Young and Beautiful, I propose a toast!

Now, this very moment! while the time's not lost;

Drink the cup of pleasures and cup of joys

For the Anguish Urn, the Old Age employs. "

71.

The Climate of the World will awry,

The evil sword shall rule by evil eye,

And you, you fools that sold the Planet's Fate

Will beg Saint Michael from the Seventh Gate...

72.

Jealousy, the ever growing Lack of Trust,

Shall engulf your mind and turn your thoughts to dust;

So burn the *fear of losing* your loved one, and end

That implanted torment that you don't understand.

73.

"Into which beauty parlor the oak has trimmed his crown?"

"Who was the make-up artist that died that green and brown?"

After One Thousand Years its colors never fade

And painter after painter still signs under its shade...

74.

- " How is it that you see and understand

What Life is all about while we pretend? "

The nightingale cried in jolly flight:

- " How is it that we' learned and that you cant? "

75.

The ruthless Force which you may call 'Revenge'

Shall hatch erratic thoughts and in plots arrange

Perhaps for 'dearest friends' to ruin and to Chase

And Tear each other, in a last embrace.

76.

Said the young man to the forest that he grew to know:

- "You're so wild and lively and I love you so,

You'll be mine forever, " and she whispered: - " Dear,

You don't have to marry me, for I am always here".

77.

If all the People the same Book would share

Creativeness would be a Climb from Where?

The starry candle-lights unnoticed in the sun

Could only stand-out if the Night is there...

78.

The nearly withered Rose, when in the house was brought

After she had her comfort and gained some strength, she thought

Her precious beauty to protect, in thorns be dressed,

And Stung the Hand that once nursed and caressed.

79.

Oh! How beguiled that Patience could get your Vigor shuttered

Into the finest ashes and thor'ly be scattered

Over the Hills of Holes and Will and Love

Until your Faith decides should you be spared or watered.

80.

And when You'll hear me knocking at your door

Asking Forgiveness and with Faith Implore

Into the Temple of Your Heart to enter, please let me in!

And I shall leave It Empty – nevermore.

" *Awe!* She's so young and pure and divine,
With marble figure dressed in velvet dress,
Her body standing ready to caress;
Oh, wintry trembling hands that cannot sign..."

The *nearly withered Rose* when in the house was brought,
After she had her *Comfort* and gain'd some Strength, she thought
Her *precious beauty* to protect - in *thorns* be *dressed*
And *Stung* the *Hand* that cured and caress'd.

81.

No matter then how flinty you may drive

Your Luck out of its corner and survive,

For Clemency encore will set you up

And throw your fate against an Ailing Ride.

82.

The Woman's sculpture made of pallid clay

Was finished by the artist the same day;

" Who's nude is that? " I asked him, and she moaned:

" I'm Venus... and ... don't touch me, get away!

83.

The Game of Love shall last when played in two

If shared fillings match, or when the cards are new;

When played by more, the King of Hearts with Diamonds Hand

Shall win your matching Queen and... that the end.

84.

Neither surprised he was, nor would he care

To raise his brows and into future stare,

But said – " *I'll see you soon* " and then asleep he went

Not saying *When* we'll meet and neither *How* nor *Where*.

85.

Myriad footprints on the sand I saw,

But none to recognize of anyone' I'd know;

Some fellows rise up their names along a castle side,

Consumed so rapid by the waves, departing with the tide. -

86.

When you believe in Love you must obey

Your Heart's Commandments in a simple way

And to its beauty bow and linger by

Lifetime after lifetime, as you may...

87.

See there, the ashes of a Fire that passed

Were swept with the first breeze and Vanished with the Gust,

But when you burn inside, they stain within

And may a lifetime flare, 'til you turn to dust.

88.

Nothing changed you see, and *Nothing's Learned*,

Wars after wars its Generations burned

And Peace was Promised as you Fight for Piece,

While History repeats as often as its pages turned.

89.

The Rule was *verbal-written* for the Age to rule,

The every single moment you embrace to see,

Even the worshiped Gods, worn out in memory

Have left to wonder, looking back at You and Me.

90.

When *Nothing Here* by *Nothing There* - scattered,

It formed a *World of Nothing* among matter,

And shows you how so least existent were

Therewith, the growing Kingdoms, which they grew forgotten.

91.

" Awe! She's so young and pure and divine

With marble figure dressed in velvet dress,

Her body standing ready to caress;

Oh! Wintry trembling hands that cannot sign ".

92.

The Clock is ticking every second: *Snip!* ;

For every moment passed, one more to whip;

The Time Inventor never had defined

When not awake, Where do these seconds Sleep?

93.

Somebody said, it would be wise to dare

The Poor and the Rich into the same affair

Since cash is blind, and care not where placed

Nor who their Master is, for all they care.

94.

The Wind of Fate is blowing strong, my dear,

So dress a warmly coat or keep it near

And it will catch you not so bare and plain

When Winter comes, to freeze your Hopes and Fears.

95.

Wonder how some *fight* and some *ignore*

Into the Present and the Future's core,

Depositing their counts within the Bank of Time,

Withdrawing once, and speechlessly withdraw.

96.

Wild geese above the water

Wake the hunters in the gutter

With their joyous free display

" Lives exposed are easy Prey "

Look in the mirror and watch the *Time Running Backwards*... What a Scold! For in your *image* you may feel You're getting *Young* when getting *Old*

The seasoned humpback beggar, lowly dressed in putrid duds,
Espied from a distant corner about a tavern's feasting crowds,
And mildly gave some cash to him and food to him I bought;
The moving crowds are vanished, where his *semblance, ever not.*

97.

Each *Reward* comes after, not before the bloom,

Look at the apple-tree against the April noon,

Its white dazzling flowers inspire the end of May

When petals after petals for its *Glorious Fruit* make room.

98.

Shaky hands and watery eyes

Through old letters wander-byes

Find the memories of the past

Where the teen years – everlasts -.

99.

And soon your paradise may seem to come

When so incited you and him shall pare into one

Near by, the scent of lilies, soft melody and wine;

Awe, pinch yourself and if it's Pain you are Alive not Gone...

100.

Do not repel when *hollow fate* is deepening,

Nor weep upon the strains of your so destined path,

Much blazing seems a Life after its Strains and Wrath;

The dread of Thunder, once departed, will be forever sleeping.

101.

When you will lose your mind and hurt someone

Beware of Yourself *after* the fault is done;

The *Voice of Conscience*, somewhere deep and somehow there

Shall come to ask: - " Where do go my friend, from here on? "

102.

The Strength of Wonder on a rustling ageless sea,

Could ignore about the surface the *wisest* You and Me,

While the cooping hand of Universe upholds our Planet's Star

Among with other Zillion Stars, important too, you see...

103.

"Oh pain, unequal pain, what have our kindred done

To drive such condemnation of suffering way beyond?

"Which power devised such fears and slept it into us

Applauding to Injustice... Pretending we have won...?"

104.

The Present, sometimes slow and sometimes fast,

Slips into the Future and the Past,

The *'very moment'* Lives within your reach,

As long as filled with touch and made to last.

105.

You know a Season when it comes, since it may warn before it shows

And once arriving stays awhile, until another comes and goes,

And so, your every day emotions announce the weather of your moods

Don't frown and sigh, they're only seasons, and Life with it, it moves, it moves.

106.

Said someone: "I'd like to climb the stairs

And be the Pinnacle of Stars somehow, up there ",

A voice cried aloud: " Even the Stars may Fall!

But, where they'll end up, is the question... Where?

108.

And You, Yourselves and Millions of your kind

With your Profound or Lost or Apathetic mind'

Will give in one by one, after your time is done

To fill the skies with moods of blue admired by the blind.

109.

The Beauty, the Softness and the Stainless Grace

Are mere common weapons for women to enlace,

Which could explode within or outright from the depths

Of their inner focus, to doom upon your pace.

110.

"How is there that fore always, the vaulting Nights and Days

Dispute their everlasting divisional displays? "

Erupted one: " What? Can't you tell,

That Twenty- Four Hours make a Full Day Spell? "

111.

Through this Botanic Garden where ' flowers drift therein

Thousand steps did echo, o' Generations, in,

Walking on the shale, whispering wows throughout

Penned in and image fading, o' Generations, out.

112.

Captive Angels suffering and scattered

Wingless souls so tender 'n' yet so mattered,

Illustrious Names commanded into Flesh

From Dust and Breathe... "Look how to ashes shuttered! "

112.

" The Winter blows to freeze December rains "

Hint'd the twigs that tapped against my panes,

And then the Spirit of the Winter calls:

" Let's see Who Stays this time... Let's see Who Goes...

113.

At the same country lodge where numerous checked in,

On the same berth and mattress which comforted Mark Twain,

Also slept you, so lost and spent, but how many of you have heard

The Voices of Tom Sawyer *calling* ...and Huckleberry Finn? ....

114.

"A shadow is always a shadow", he said,

Confusing an image wherever is led

The way it arrived, the same way shall go,

And Nothing behind it shall change the image so... "

115.

"Oh Love, how is it then that you pretend to heal

The deepest wounds instilled in us, and figure then to steal

Our only hope, eternally branded into our souls and senses

Immortal faith and dazzled smiles, broken on false pretenses! "

116.

Compare not the very moment, for the next one could easily bring

For some King to be a beggar and some Pilgrim be a King;

Look upon yourself and question if you awe yourself or not,

Life is Hope, a String of Wonders, that you may work at, knot by knot.

117.

"How many sweethearts have you embraced with winning love and care

That you would now like to recall, just for a moment' spare

To *Hold* and *Taste* and *Feel* that heat and *Melt* within their souls? "

You shot your eyes and call their names, but *where* they are, *who* knows? "

118.

The seasoned humpback beggar, lowly dressed in putrid duds

Espied from a distant corner about the tavern's feasting crowds

And blandly gave some cash to him and food to him I brought

The moving crowds were vanished, but his semblance ever not.

119.

Some Proof of the Universal Love you've reached and reaped

Into your heart part emptiness eagerly pour it down and dipped,

Grew therein the vibrant splendor of a lovie-dovie crop

Whose indoors are swept by cherished, piece by piece and drop by drop.

120.

The water trickled from the fountain's crest

Along with thousand years which passed to rest;

" How many lovers by its side set voiceless hopes

Of memories and kissing lips, forever pressed? "

121.

You and Yourself, the *Both of You*, be strong,

Awake from weakness! and turn what's Right from Wrong,

The *'friends'* you thought you had, now let you down

So, tear up this page and write a better song.

122.

Of what it was, a little but remained,

The most of thy experience 'twas ordained;

" Whatever's written it will come to pass " quoth he

A thousand years ago and his words never waned.

123.

Among the crowds I roam and lost I get

And raft among the shades not rotted yet,

Of knowing not where going, hence afar

I think my *alter ego* have been let.

124.

Youth? Just a *teasing pattern* shaped by our life's display

With Everlasting Feelings of an Eternal Force,

Impressed throughout the Vail of Time, then to Divorce '

For never to re-marry, until you're Old and Gray.

125.

Of Instant Money many a word was told,

Since the beholder never could behold,

For cursed the pelf obtained by easy gains

To which so many their souls have sold.

126.

The *Greatest Show on Earth* may have begun,

When *Cash* and *Putrid* share the World as *One*,

The Opera of Mankind will erupt to see

At Genesis horizon, Apocalypse for dawn.